# A West Coast Psalter

# A West Coast Psalter

Poems by

Maggie Mackay

*To Susan,*
*yours one,*
*Maggie Mackay*
*January 2021*

Cover design by Shay Culligan
Cover artwork by Claire Jefferson

ISBN: 978-1-952326-88-2

Kelsay Books
502 South 1040 East, A-119
American Fork, Utah, 84003

For the Hyslops and the McGibbons

# Acknowledgments

Some of the poems in this collection have appeared in the following journals and anthologies:

*Ink, Sweat & Tears:* "What Every Rusholme Housemaid Wants"

*Atrium:* "Dolls of Chaos," "Sell Your Petticoat and Go to Sea"

*Obsessed With Pipework:* "The Library,1963," "Baudelaire in Govan," "Spoon"

*As Above, So Below:* "Belonging," "You Can Feel the Freedom Coming On," "A Change Gonna Come"

*The Curlew:* "Ballantrae in its Heyday"

*Domestic Cherry 6:* "Anxiety," "On Breathing Nitrous Oxide," "Women Do Not Count"

*Three Drops from a Cauldron:* "Homecoming," "Fitch," "The Glaistig," "Cailleach," "My Father as a Zephyr," "Divination"

*White Noise & Ouija Boards anthology:* "Haunted by Annie"

*Celebrating Change:* "War Bride"

*The Screech Owl:* "The Patternmaker, Govan Shipyards,1915"

*Writers' Café Magazine:* "Muzzled," "Dressmaker," "African Dust," "The Tree of Tales"

*I am not a Silent Poet:* "Slavery in all Shapes"

*Southlight 21:* "Cantation to Henryson"

*One Hand Clapping*: a version of "Void"

*Algebra of Owls:* "Rite of Passage"

*Silver Birch Press:* "Wool in the Grease"

*Reach:* "Chiaroscuro"

*Bonnie's Crew:* "Growing into my Mum," "Touch," "Two Hour Prescription"

*Noble Dissent Anthology:* "Counterfire"

*Bees Breakfast Anthology:* "A Paisley Buddy's Chant"

*Paper Swans Press:* The Little Book of Anger, "Jamaican Macabre"

*Ledbury Poetry Festival, The Physic Garden Anthology:* "Perfume"

*Hedgehog Poetry Press:* "Mellon Udrigle," "A Lead Mark in a Box"

*Contemporary Haibun Online:* "Owning the Past"

*The Everyday Poet Anthology:* "Summertime"

*For the Silent Anthology:* "Hognap"

*Laldy:* "Bewitched"

*The Blue Nib:* "A Spell in the Asylum"

# Contents

# Sell the Petticoat and Go to Sea

*It's a gey wondrous place and I'm lucky for tae see it and live.*
—George Bissett, great-great-grandfather carpenter,1866


Bleachfields spread in Clydeside sun.
Whitening sheets blink,
ballooning like tides, like sails,
as Jacobina's man clips his fortune
to a passage out of Greenock,
destined for the far east of the globe.
George is ship's carpenter, adventurer
to places she'd never know, to sunken reefs,
uncharted water, monsoon sky, coral rock.

Here sits her little life on earth,
a China junk on the windowsill,
bairns to raise and poems to pencil.
She writes of herself,
not the cutter or stitcher of silk,
but as the nation's spy,
flying a hot air balloon across the Continent.

# Owning the Past

On a spring afternoon close to Easter I'm following a dry mud trail towards a cluster of derelict cottages. They huddle below a lead mine's chimney stack rising into Ayrshire sky. Boards secure the empty door spaces. Between the gaps I spy Victorian tiled fireplaces, their colours dimmed by time, the half ruins of lost seasons. Traces of potato lazy beds are pencilled in the overgrowth by the Garryhorn Burn. Rolling green stretches to the horizon, a tranquil ghost witness of the Killing Times, the hounding which outran the people and their freedoms.

Claverhouse redcoats
swords harvesting bloody flesh
stone cross stands, Kells dusk.

# Wool in the Grease

It's late June, no rain forecast today.
A heat haze rises over Ballantrae Bay,
misting the watercolour wash of sea and sky.

By the pen I flip the Cheviot between my legs,
prop her shoulders between my knees.

Next, I steady the weight as her legs push,
then point stock-still into the air, her belly exposed.

Sweat begins to drip into my eyes, salty and blinding.
Dad whispers instructions, *don't nick, mind the teats.*

I balance his wrought iron shears in my right hand,
pushing the left hard flat against her smoothed skin.

She bleats in protest. Fleece piles around her shape
like a cloak unwinding into a creamy white skin.

# Carzield

It's a still life. Witness a man, his allotment,
daily chores, seasons demarking duties,
a lodge, tied dwelling, three children.
Wood smoke, hedgehogs, fox turds,
egg collecting at dawn, bulbs wrapped
in the Big House's refuse newsprint.

Far below foundations and soil
Roman military life remains to be found,
papyrus, listing names of soldiers, marshalled at the lost fort,
who clatter samian pottery, bought and removed from Gaul.
These men wash in the tiled bathhouse, crack bawdy jokes,
patrol the northern Antonine Wall.

James Emslie, gardener, inks his name in copperplate for the
census.

# Dressmaker

Mr Foulds, her landlord, loves the woods of Dalry,
Dundeugh, Polmaddy, Clattershaws. Their roots underpin his
bones. He rustles.

He speaks of bullfinch, canopy. Broadleaf flutters and transpiration
spills from his lips.
Folk seek him out, eased by his love of thrush, goldcrest, ash,
dunnock.

He champions the beetle in the crevice of a rotted tree, the tree
creeper hidden in bark.
The seasons ooze from him in patterns of colour spun from
midsummer to midwinter.

Maggie crooks around the kitchen door with his jacket altered to fit
his failing limbs.
A pair of brown eyes, his grandson's, meet hers. She stops a while
as usual for a chat.

He is a young gardener from some grand house down south,
beginning his trade.
The talk is of parkland, not forest, an icehouse, pineapple pits. She
relaxes.

The men argue the worth of asparagus, the forcing and art of
grafting,
Pippin and Hessel, their weights that summer, a lake rising from
natural springs.

Next comes her favourite, a rose garden of two hundred varieties,
then orchids.
She sews a new seam, marriage, beyond her father's holding,
beyond Dalry.

# War Bride

I board a steamship wider than the Waverley.
Salty, saltier than the Clyde, the Atlantic is pulling me west.

Gales shower-bathe me, one of three hundred brides this week,
dashing me over swell to Canada, stun me
with the triple mirrors of Northern lights, icebergs and trade winds.

For goodness sake, me, a Scot
in the wake of Vikings, polar explorers and refugees.

# The Patternmaker, Govan Shipyards, 1915

*You would have loved him*
my mother insisted
*your Granddad was a real gentleman.*

He ran lines along
2D sketches, stacked images
one on top of another,
switched to 3D and back.
Give him a sketch, an ink drawing.

His pen shaped calculations,
three or four drawings on top of each other.
Mr Elite - upon whom the life of a ship rested.

Brown overcoated he held sway in the shop,
awash in pine shavings.
He cut moulds for castings.
The heaving and lifting was hard graft.
Destroyers, minesweepers, Transatlantic liners.

At Calside he cut and cast lives for his three sons
and, in time, for his daughter,
three graduates and a post mistress,
a Paisley pattern rich with possibilities.
His keen eye and knack with maths repeat in her.

He knew the properties of metals.
His companion was the steel contraction rule.
He's caught in a still,
three-piece suit, pocket watch, bunnet,
blinking in the Clyde shallows.

# The Black Sheep

He props his old Raleigh against the sandstone,
lifts the latch. It clunks.
He steps into childhood.

First, Tommy's fiddle strings greet him
with Ye Banks and Braes
and, a rare treat, Harriet's push-pull melody
on buttons and bellows,
its Spanish latticed wood
polished silk-sleek.

Ah, he stops stock-still in the hall
caught by George's cheer,
those deep chords.
Auntie holds her contralto note
for the rattle of dice rolling a six,
the clatter up a ladder,
another snake's fangs frustrated.

He shivers, still draped in November chill.
The company draws him in,
like a tidal wave, swallows him whole.

# Monday

is prune-fingers, purple with chill.
Her sons fight on the Somme today.
All morning, she's pummelled
in tin tubs with yon washboard,
forced linen through a steam-shrouded mangle.
Lifebuoy suds agitate those bloomers,
cloud her mind. She spots the raindrop,
darts through scullery door,
a fired arrow aimed at the path,
straight into the taut line, catapults backwards
in a solid bounce heavy on damp grass,
she a rolling barrel of plumpness,
stymied by the drying green pole.
The wooden prop shudders, tips like a caber
to lie against her hip. Shirts, socks, pants, sheets
shoogle under grey canopy,
now streaked by blades of grass and boot prints.

# Void

Father hanged himself
perhaps above
the washhouse mangle,
or in the orchard maybe,
dead weight dressed in apple blossom.

You're wondering if I miss him,
if I miss his hand on my arm,
if his voice is fading.
It's in the sparrow's call,
ten chisel clangs,
a bicycle bell.

# Divination

The weight of her ghost rests in this key
and I've given her name to our third lass, Jessie.
A fistful of iron, it's our good luck charm,
this wee house, its rose beds, weathering glass.

Let it unlock smiles, bar tears,
welcome song, yoke strangers.
Let it grow love with the breaking of bread,
and I pray it wards off a child's passing,
keeps whooping cough from the schuil gate,
repels thieves from the cot when night imps mass.

# Flotsam

Everyone is
faking it,
nursing twisted guts
while moist eyes count
minutes to anchor away.
The *Scandinavian* sways
against harbour wall
as Jessie climbs
the plank out of the now
into a new.

A passport,
tight clutches,
big brother James guides
feathered hats and suited
friends weaving zigzags
between the Clyde-rooted,
the seaborne migrants.
Waves on waves linger beyond
the curved earth.

# Sisters' Song

*Dear Margaret*
I settle by these River Forks, settle and remain,
fight off mosquitoes from stagnant ponds.
I drown in Norwegian vowels,
*Ææ, Øø and Åå,*
babbled by Helga, Astrid, Gudrun and more.
Today is Syttende Mai, their day
and the air speaks in tongues.
Weldon's waving flags of a different
red, white and blue.

I've grown fond of nature's sounds,
the white throated sparrow, humming wind.
Night thunderstorms paint silver
over our homestead roof. Lightning prongs stab the sky.
Mornings, the crack-crunch, George's sawing,
and in the silences, I hear the Old World.
I clutch to familiar words beyond
wave-wash and the lurch of the westward ship.
They pull-push me, sing of this land,
a land with no shoreline.

*Dear Jessie*
I don't know how to say I wish I were you.
My passport, Empire blue, could be a golden ticket,
if, …and the world was un-topsy-turvied.
My case brims with stories
and cotton, needles and threads
and the stuff of a spinster.
One more Paisley night and the westwarding starts.

You speak of novelty, sweat, homesickness,
of heat and blisters. You seem too busy to think.
I hear the familiar mill horn, my Singer trundle.
These days my ankles crack
as they flex back and forth on the treadle.
But I must turn around with my heavy heart,
so many haste-ye-backs with only
your welcome smile, my loss never spoken of.
I see him in your George,
who fills the photograph frame,
muscle and grin, log cabin and crops.

# Spoon

Margaret would laugh
to discover they were to be heirlooms
tarnished by salt and prairie big skies.

Jessie packs the spoon for her sea voyages,
east to St Petersburg's mills,
forever to Prince Albert's farms.
A scotch broth memento, it is the one piece of home
she can stroke with her calloused fingertips.
It stirs up a clatter of ashets,
the filling brew-bubble on the stove.
She hears Mother's giggle,
Father's long shadow hangs by the door.

Beside it lists a battered box of coffee spoons.
Granny loved their black bean ends.
Now they lodge in migrant saucepans
where the Atlantic sway cannot reach.
They surge away from the blethers
and chink of Sunday afternoon china.

# A Spell in the Asylum

Dear departed Mrs Latta mists over
as I wave, ghost-flesh melted into nothing,
the only almost-mother in my earthly world.
Arm in arm we'd walk and shop on Paisley's streets.

My gaggle of babes is somewhere,
in another woman's kitchen or head to toe asleep.
Until my name returns to me, I'm in Bedlam.

That girl stitched into Mrs Latta's needlework
hung above the marital bed haunts me,
a framed, gazing statue. She is me,
prisoner of others, a voyeur of my life.

Spiders suspend from the glass, dance with their prey,
consume my brain in criss-cross webs,
and my body ripples purpled twitches.
White lilies chatter.

I'm falling through a moving floor;
grief for Mrs Latta clings to my petticoat shreds.
Someone has painted my hands with bloodied streaks.
The laundry tubs bubble. My baby's skin, my wedding linen,
the sheen of copper pans are alien now.

# Anxiety

is Auntie's Venus Flytrap,
prize-winner carnivore, her particular
hothouse plant potted near her Singer.
Each tremble-twitch she makes
sets leaves in action.
Hairs detect prey, her stress
the mock-motion of a beetle
into that space of danger,
snap-shut tight after twenty seconds.
Venus digests innards
in a land unplotted by any earthly cartographer,
inflicts a ten-day catalyst upon her nerves.

# Baudelaire in Govan

My uncle gazes back at me
sightless through the window in the morgue.
Grave and kind, he was no bletherskite
sandpapered by the war's blasted grit.
Slumped on his lap at death
was a volume of Baudelaire in French,
paired with tumbler drops of Famous Grouse.

Baudelaire gazes into the lens, towards Nadar,
his lover's ex-lover, yet his friend.
His face is a stare, three times removed from us,
mind, negative, and positive,
seeded in contempt for the photograph.
Angled and suited in blackest of black, and pale,
he reveals only the left eye, a pierce-spear
into light. The right hides
in the dark of the far side of his head,
hairline receding, hair tickling an earlobe.

Grave and still, who would suspect him
a fugitive from the norm,
an outsider witness to metropolitan life,
a poet of sound and symbol,
and a worry to his mother.

# Sharing a Bed

A search on Google Earth,
one window, a wee sandstone square,
Nessie and her aunt within its frame;
snores, chat, song, secrets, first days.

Then, a gas lamp flicker, tick-tock chime
while the day crowds the bed -
tip tap wired telegrams, posted gifts,
worst news, good news,
the dash and whirr of Auntie's sewing machine,
black ink blotters, date stamps,
firebombs Nessie fled from in dead of night,
a 'goodnight', a stretch, sigh, a 'darling',

talk of choir practice, of the latest South Church sermon,
of Cousin Irene in Canada, Auntie's voyage,
her passport and the 1950s wedding dresses,
the man at Nessie's work who wants her,
and never about the one who let her down.

# Chiaroscuro

It's a thunderstorm in July. In nightie and baffies,
you are a stone pillar in the darkest-dark of the larder,
a ribbon of shiver. You are humming Psalm 121.

Shelves of familiar scent calm you, bring light.
You imagine mixing flour, eggs and butter
into Happy Birthdays, your children's giggles,
faces at the kitchen door.

It all comes back: Lyle's Golden Syrup, tins of Bartlett pears,
a red Carnation cream can, John West salmon flakes,
Bird's vanilla-podded custard powder,
a rustle-up on a lazier day, the pipe smoke tang.
It all comes back.

You imagine stirring tablet mix, drop pancakes
and ice Sunday's teatime buns,
fingers licking bowls, pans rattling on the rack.

You keek around the door into dawn's blether.

# The Library, 1963

It's a great game
finding you.
Up and down the aisles
I creep on tippy-toe,
threading through coat hems,
serenaded by the whack
of bindings on counter,
the silt of page turning,
as the station-size clock marks
the passing hours, lost forever.
Coughs and murmurs ignore me,
only me moving through,
and there you stand,
trilby angled into the page,
and you say, as always,
*Ah, there you are.*

# My Father as a Zephyr

Lightest of all things,
he blows in light of a perpetual spring,
scatters the salty Clyde with early summer breezes,
with seaweed fronds on soft foam,
fruit of our childhood holidays.
His soft stirring smile greets aquamarine.
His wind-song dances on fiddle strings, sotto.
The west wind restores dear ones
with a tease, a coorie-in, a purr.

# Perfume

May thoughts of the lily drift,
beyond clay red rope edging,
neon green scrolls and tiny white bells
shy and arching in the shade,
bring a return of happiness,
steady the rhythm of my broken heart.

My mother is walking into our garden.
She curves over the border, as if in prayer,
as the scent bursts across her face,
a whisper kiss of lost childhood springtimes
and good luck posies in bulbous vases,
warming, even under this gloomy Scottish sky.

# Growing into my Mum

It's crept up on me,
her portrait
across my face,
my hazel eyes,
her serious gaze
when I'm hatted,
preparing for winter.

# Touch

On New Year's Day, our last to be,
I sit by Mum, bodies a nerve apart.
She fiddles with the cooling salmon on her plate.
I soothe the flat of her hand, paper skin.
We smile, eyes meeting. That's enough.
You are everything to me.

# Summertime

*after Chris Powici*

My mother is clearing dandelions
in the rockery at the front of the house.
Trowel in hand, she has just rocked back
to greet a neighbour on the street
who waits by the gate for a blether.
Soon she will come through the open door,
to pour tea and watch *The Chase.*
But for now, she walks down the stone path,
her hair bleached by days of sun.
So, I imagine.

# Belonging

When my time comes,
folk will find it
among the bits and bobs,
toffee hammer, dice, harmonica,
penny whistle, Dinky car.


That last March day
when they came to clear the villa,
I slipped the key into my bag,
cast iron, Victorian, rusted,
familiar from childhood,
solid as our family life.


Just holding its weight,
I am their daughter, home.
I hear the turn, ker-clunk
and the house sleeps.
I hear the ker-clunk,
the day begins.

# Mary Queen of Scots Doesn't Get Her Head Chopped Off

She's our new librarian, this Ms Stuart.
A natural redhead, she sweeps towards us
in her vintage gown, like a barge on the River Seine.
She claims she is a true Scot. Doesn't sound at all like us.
Who let her in? She's lost her way to the French class.

She whispers prayers each study period
and bans our dog-eared young adult fiction.
The spines split like walnuts as they hit the floor.
She spits a *sacré bleu*. We offer her Google.

We snigger at a Virgin and Child poster.
She plays a lute, a lute, who's heard of that?
Her embroidery sessions drive Miss Murdoch
to breaking needles on the Singer Scholastic.

We sit at her knee, like ladies-in-waiting.
She tells fairy tales, family stories of book collections,
of a Europe once upon a time.
We learn about harps and Latin,
a Dauphin, and plots.

She'd make a wicked history teacher.

# This Woman of Riddle's Court

I am from a time/before/
soot and slums stole/
this space/from delicate matter/
infused by a man's vision/
from out of Elizabeth/
from Baltic amber/I am
out of a masque/strange enigma/
tall as an oak/born to walk/
these floors/to bring art/
to the Scots. Mother
of a doomed king/I stand/
straight-spined/invincible/
in my George Heriot pearls/
and red cuff and collar silk.

# Counterfire

The shriek bursts from a single end;
'Ma brave man took yon King's shilling.
A dinae hae the rent ye seek.' Stramash in the close.

Wi that, Mary birls her rioty fitba rattle,
marshals lassies in kitchens, steamies and back courts,
wi hails of furnace setting fire in soft bellies.

In every window of every house of every street after street
hang placards, black-inked 'WE ARE NOT REMOVING'.
Bang drums, blow whistles, clatter pot lids. Keep watch. Ring yon
    bell.

It's a battle of wills now. Bat-bat-battlely-bat wi landlords
for 'our men are fighting the Prussians in Germany
and we are fighting the Prussians of Partick.'

March, march, gie it laldy. Mind, wear your Sunday best.
Whack those bowler-hatted sheriffs wi mealy flour,
rot frae the middens, peasemeal, wet claes, or worse.

A few hundred feet apart, he smells them, puzzles at the strange
    accent.
Stepping onto No Man's Land, Ypres Salient,
(we won't fire if you dinna) Sergeant Baker retrieves dead
    comrades,

then joins free-for-all football wi the Germans. Nae referee.
It's Christmas Eve. Night has fallen—no shots today or the next or
    the next.
*Stille Nacht* floats across the mud thick air. Glamourie.

Tussle, tackle, scramble. We're twenty thousand strong now.
Sardines packed layers strong. We want justice, pre-war rents.
Lloyd George, change the law. NOW. Rat-rat-rattely-rattle.

## Slavery in all Shapes

The tumbling lassie is what they call me.
I've no other name. I'm a little girl.
My joints are stiff with dancing,
in all shapes on the stage
at Mr Reid's travelling show.
He oils them every day.
Tumble, tumble,
three hundred and thirty years ago.
Look hard, look twice now
at the car wash lads and nail bar lassies.
Look hard, take a tumble, give shelter,
for forced labour they may be
and under Scotland's law
we have no slaves. I was made free.

# What Every Rusholme Housemaid Wants

*Sarah, get yourself to the boating lake. They take a turn each day.*


Granted an afternoon's relief from dust and grates,
Cook wheeshes me out the basement door to Platt Fields
where the lake is an ocean of rowing boat bob
and a brass band is playing 'When the Saints Go Marching In'.

Soft smiling Miss Esther Roper, grave Miss Eva Gore-Booth,
my secret crush, I blush at the thought
of a glimpse, the couple arm-in-arm,
pinch-waisted, faces moon-framed by spectacles.

Ah, see them now,
by purple lavender, lily of the valley snow,
lime trees fanning in the breeze.
I catch their conversation,
snatch words, 'rights' 'flower sellers' 'suffrage'.

Mother's always telling me to mind my ways.

# A Lead Cross in a Box

Witness women scrub sweat out of cotton
by the Nankokwe's current rush through forest,
while the men brew beer, take shelter in the shade.
*

Harriet, kitchen maid at Linthouse Mansion
scrubs tatties, heaves jelly pans.
'I work hard six and a half days a week.
The words 'rights' and 'votes' fill my waking day.'
*

Segregated by the male vote to a separate seating area
at the first World's Anti-Slavery Convention of 1840,
Lucretia Mott calls to us through the centuries,
'I long for the day my sisters will rise,
and occupy the sphere
to which they are called by their high nature and destiny.'
*

My dear wife's place is at home.
A gentlewoman,
she does not possess
the capacity to make such choices.
Parliament would be a ruin.
*

Esther Roper went out and about,
to Manchester women in factories and at home.
'Women pay taxes, contribute to the economy.
The least men in Parliament can do is give you a vote,
and a say on laws affecting your working conditions.'
*

Helen cracked the whip.
The Royal Albert Hall saw burly men
hurl themselves on me,
smother my mouth with their coarse hands,
carry me bodily and with violence.
Lies in the press and Lloyd George's disdain.
*

Woodrow felt an icy breath on the back of his neck,
thinking about the 1912 election,
not exactly a landslide,
and if enough of the four million women voters
—and maybe some of their husbands or brothers—
turned against him, he might lose in 1916...
Maybe it was time to talk to his colleagues on the Hill.
*

In 2017 a Bolton woman was asked
'Will you vote in future?'
'I really don't know.
What is certain though,
is politics is going to have to get a hell
of a lot more interesting
if I, and my girlfriends, are going
to put a cross in a box.'
*

Emily Davidson falls under trampling hooves.

# Women Do Not Count

Evaders, new women, missing wives go
ice skating in Aldwych, hide in sheds, in haylofts all night.
The March of the Women greets the vanished tonight.
All night they protest in Trafalgar Square, dance at campaign
 parties.
On the form Dorothy Bowker pens her chutzpah.

There's a secret password exchange at Denison House
where suffragettes huddle in rooms, a garret and cellars.
Charlotte Marsh gives a reading of Ibsen's forbidden Ghosts.
In the House of Commons Emily Davison dines
on meat lozenges and lime juice until she is discovered, recorded.

# Crying the Banns, 1915

Hattie, heavy with wedding plans,
looks out at Paisley Canal Street
as the train draws in, looks for
her signalman betrothed.

She speaks better than she writes,
spinning a pencilled letter to her *dear Jim*
with Mrs Love's children around her feet
and house removals on her mind.

Try at Sugar House Lane, she suggests.
The Glebe Refinery crosses her mind.
Raw sugar. Filter presses. Charcoal kilns.

Marriage - a mutchkin of sugar,
a filter press of tact, a furnace of hot affection.

# Muzzled

*What becometh a woman best, and first of all? Silence. What second?*
*Silence. What third? Silence. What fourth? Silence.*
*Yea, if a man should aske me till Domes daie I would still crie silence,*
*silence.*

—Thomas Wilson, The Arte of Rhetorique, 1560


With a flourish and a musical beat
the local blacksmith softens the iron;
a scold's bridle for the town authority.

Bessie Telfer brankit for her voice,
fixed to the Mercat Cross for one hour,
Dorothy Waugh, Quaker preacher of Carlisle,
bridled for three hours,
a collar and stone weight iron strip splayed
across her face at the nose,
one sip of air at a time, no room for words,
an iron arch ear to ear over her head,
one more bar below the nose,
or two or three, a bit between her lips
to fix her tongue, stippled with spikes,
up, down and back,
metal nettles to cut the palate too;
whipped as they drove her from town to town.

# You Can Feel the Freedom Coming On

Nameless women and girls are spinning
in a cochineal heat, air thick
with the never-ending revolutions
of Glasgow cotton looms.
This heat smears skin
like a poultice of crushed bugs
and sweated labour of slavery.
One of them mouths *unity, lassies;*
in the yard another speaks of
the burning of Nottingham Castle
thirty years before.

# A Change is Gonna Come

*Blue Plaque 33 Gilmore Place*


Frederick Douglass hums an old tune,
an old familiar from slavery times.
He stands before the mirror, free to see
the radical reformer, unseeing the slave on the run,
never unseeing the fugitive within his soul.
*Right is of no sex, truth is of no colour.*
Douglass speaks of all freedoms.

One row of terraced stone and two hundred years;
a girl grew up on this same street, on the same side,
raised to be independent and equal.

Dread and danger are different countries now,
scars, living memory of his bloodied flesh.
Dark-matter-chains are feathers around his wrists.
Leading, he finds a new bravery;
*send back the blood-stained money.*
At his desk he writes, *All is smooth.*
*I am treated as a man, an equal brother.*

# Haunted by Annie

Into the dark of history, I walk, fall down Mary King's Close, like
Alice-in-Wonderland, towards narrow space, walls to the left and
right of me caked in arsenic coverings. I hear the song of a bairn
called Annie, her cry carried down the centuries, a plea for relief
from her plague agony. Eerie light flickers, electric white.
Once a marshy, dank Nor Loch, this underworld is a labyrinth of
claustrophobia, the air steeped in noxious gas seeping from
medieval effluence. My footsteps echo in this world of
hallucination, pull me closer to weird dreams and chill.
The babe Annie dead
in the gloom, canker blighted,
mourns a winter's tale

# Cantation to Henryson

On this morning's faux pilgrimage
under a sky of four seasons
she hears herself talking to him in Anglo Scots;
*you'd be fine wi its soonds, Maister.*

She might write a royal stanza tale
of the silent things within the soul,
honey-gold knuckled, under-toned
by twenty-first century irony.

*Quhen Aries, in middis of the Lent, soaks
me with schouris of hail.*

Through Medusa twists of trees,
she stumbles down stepped remains
of the coffin walk along the dyke,
its sage cloak wrapped around churchyard bones,
where a stray mandible once lay weathered.

She calls Henryson up out of the sea haar.

*Pull me out of the quair and into the now.
Stop my heart, Spreit.*

And, that moon-drenched night, eavesdrops
on the goose feather scratch of his quill
blended with the Forth wave-roll
of a printing press as it tramps the shingle.

*Your ain tale, clootit an steekit,
you've made a comeback, ye ken
—the critics cry you, writer o the purest Scots.*

God speid, Makar.

# A Paisley Buddy's Chant

Rise on Renfrew thermals
cairied by fire an helium,
oor haunds straucht tae heiven,
caught atween whit we witness
and whit we imagine the land ance tae be.

Let's glide ower ancestral earth
whaur dreich Atlantic creep nursed
Auntie Jessie's rattling, prattling dance,
cotton mill thread spun intae yon Paisley pattern.

Tent tae grandfaither Tam's ghost-gruff voice
as he cuts patterns in the Fairfield yaird,
afore an empire crumbled tae iron filings.
Hear the wind whizz wi clang an burn
o metal, the trundle boom o looms.

Blink at river sparks, sea watter
coils an white horses in the Firth.
Measure quilted strip fields,
stroke Gleniffer Braes wi sighs,
the living green o a west coast spring,
magnets tae earth ye close tae hame.

Rise, float ower ruined towers an turrets,
Kilbarchan threads, a salmon weir.
Tell a yarn o brown trout fishing on the Gryffe.
Shiver at the alien gargoyle gurning
frae a spout o Paisley Abbey stane.

# Ballantrae in its Heyday

On a quiet bay, *Baile na Tràgha* on the Carrick coast,
on the River Stinchar's tidal pools,
a place of excellent salmon beats and trout fishing.
Shingle-sand lapping Ailsa Craig, Arran and Kintyre.
Sky thick with offshore divers, Manx shearwaters, gannets.
Harbour crowded by barrels of white herrings, beside cod, ling,
    and hake,
fish-curers' song, coopers' hammers,
boat pitch by stone-worn jetty.
Noted as a smugglers' haunt, a rude and primitive
place of brandy and revolutionary ideas hefted into rocky coves,
hill tenant shepherds blown ruddy with sea salt in their beards.

# Rite of Passage

Girlie-girls, city-bred on the scheme, turn out,
suitcases past sell-by date, strapped with belts.
Kohl lines frame Cleopatra eyes,
allium spikes of spray-stiff hair quiver
slick with mousse, and then there's the damson perm.
A wail of guttural *nae way* fills the bus.

Bedtime unravels. A cluster of smiles
shows off a photograph of a soldier,
tucked into a layer of grey-white undies,
the boyfriend, *he's braw, eh, Miss?*

Alarm clocks rattle, sleepy-heads mumble,
*what's this, eh? where's ma Coco Pops, eh?*
Life jackets, canoes, Inuit style, slumber on the shore.
Water whooshes towards their feet. Eyes widen.

*Nae way* goes up the chant,
*nae way* at the very thought.

Loch Morar waits, glint under the widest blue.
Paddle hard, Atlantic bound,
never coming back. *This is magic, Miss.*

# Mellon Udrigle

Waiting for you, unannounced, beyond a high moor, is a tinkling name
on a road with no number, a secret, secret of dolphins, whale

and the occasional sheep; beyond the dunes, Camas a'Charaig's stretch
of snow-sand strokes your feet, and there at the gloaming, be seduced by

the sea of liquid gold. Midas would envy you this treasure trove of elements.
Your eyes will pop at views of Suilven, Coigach, An Teallach, Gruinard Bay.

Here rests a place of sea mist and shimmer, ever-changing, every moment,
a place where fairies and kelpies might just make magic,

where you find only a few cottages, caravans and a telephone box,
beauty to dream away the day. Wheesht, it's a secret.

# Hognap

I'm a gobbler of slugs,
beetles, caterpillars, snails,
a digger, a climber, a swimmer.
Dusk heralds my 'to do' time,
spring, summer, autumn.

By Halloween I'm a fat forager
for leaves in suburban gardens,
wilted countryside bracken,
reeds by a bittern's hiding ground.
I'm a busy builder in a hidden pocket,
maybe a hedgerow, tree root,
under logs, under sheds.

Locate my hibernaculum, if you can,
insulated, watertight, fit for winter torpor,
a refuge for my heartbeat of twenty per minute.

Do not disturb.

# Bewitched

During the light, day after day,
Owl waits, tucked in down,
invisible, in the fork of the oak.
Keeper of secrets, keeping
his counsel, he's a master at that
while the human world sleeps.
Night guardian of the movements
of tiny mammals and fish
beneath the river shallows
now he slumbers as if in a stupor.
Salmon is heading home,
like a sleek arrow from a bow,
after thousands of miles in the ocean.
At the full moon,
a homecoming trill and splash
of feather and scales,
lovers again on the River Tay.

# Homecoming

The house slumps in the smelt of hail and drought,
its gates at the angle of two Pisa twists
splayed by rust's hunger and a two generation
memory scorch where you once played tag.
Red kites skirt the stone, guarded by ghost-whispers;
the stamp of a boy scout boundary march.

Crooked wood casts its spell
in a pool of spokes, daggered grey and brown.
The door presses close, a crizzled mirror
to my questioning face. Shudder of dust hovers,
a blur of feather slips over a beam.
I view the tangle you brought to this place.

Splinters of our lives stop me where I falter.
Pale framed squares hint at booty and heirlooms,
those Flangs and Solsons we hated but
you claimed as fallbacks for a rainy day,
when we'd wear Arctic furs,
and the wine vault oozed ruby blood.

The doll's house sits on the top landing
with the fort and the castle and King Arturo.
Cast as a relic, he folded flat into a Steptoe cart
when you dumped this place and ran.
I thought I'd rediscover smiles here,
a trace of us, of being cast free.

I was treading a dance of polkas and reels,
keeping watch over the boy I was,
childhood boxed and squeezed.
As the moment blurs, I watch
plaided crofters flee from the moor.

# African Dust

Take Hill Road, Malawi's most scenic route,
and wind east towards Golomoti's bustle
on hairpin bends and gradients,
snatch a speckle-glisten
of the ninth largest lake on earth.

Then, at the halfway stretch, to the west,
follow the track into Mganja,
where, on your map, you meet a single rectangle,
the school playground. Hear its wail on winter dust
under giant pylons, wired from Blantyre to Lilongwe.
Boys kick a plastic bag football.

Witness women washing sweat out of cotton
in the Nankokwe's current, rushing through forest.
No legend for the laughter, the water pump's gush,
connected back to front, nor the maize monitor,
the one electrical connection to the world.
Forest howls wild beast, star-beds sparkle and wink.
Girls, invisible, scavenge for firewood, wait for marriage.

No cartographer maps chants, campfires, or drums
vibrating down bicycle tracks, bodies pulsing.
There's no coded symbol for traders' stalls,
their vibrant fabrics of earth and fire,
only blurred images of corrugated roofs,
orange trees amid dustbowls,
a deserted maize mill.

# Dolls of Chaos

Somewhere consigned to shadow
in the nervous system of my childhood brain
a collection of paper dolls huddle,
thrawn Shikigami beings,

one feline-featured with retractable claws,
whiskers varnished snow-white,
another on twenty-four-hour watch,
yellow wings tucked into raggedy coal-black lining,

the third, a mousey creature of tiny ears
and pencil-thin body, waistcoat of velvet-grey
and boss of those three, Fox Trot,
fur etched with blood sticky plots.

They cause mischief to haunt every hour.
Cut-outs from my infancy,
they mess with human heads,
spin them full circle.

Let me give orders,
let them steal, spy and track
the bullies, deceivers,
you enemies of my curious world.

# Jamaican Macabre

It will be my pleasure to poison Mr Rae
as him eats in the Great House.
The fools, Lord Belmore and Sir Willoughby Cotton
dance the Creolian hop a la Mustee.

I slave in his kitchens,
my belly fired after him rape mi in the scullery
like I was his peaberry fruit.
His boasts ride on fiddle jigs into the valley
where my baby sleeps.

# The Laboratory for the Elixir of Love

Should you look for me, I'm at Callanish,
encircled by its standing stones, keeping guard.
I've swallowed a star, drunk in a blue moon.
My workbench is ancient oak, etched with hieroglyphs,
scattered with pomegranate seed, apple filings,
my microscope, Petri dishes and well-worn gloves.
This air is infused with powder,
the powdery warm juicy scent of the fruit of love.
I'm implanting its alphabet into our gene sequence,
a cryptogram bacterium, feat of wild imaginings.

# On Breathing the Nitrous Oxide

*Not in the ideal dreams of wild desire,*
*Have I beheld a rapture wakening form,*
*My bosom burns with no unhallowed fire,*
*Yet is my cheek with rosy blushes warm.*
                    —Humphry Davy


I googled genetic, found epigenetic,
truncated receptor, was baffled by biallelic.
Out of the muddle, I discovered
how to be Humphry Davy,
the scientist who loved
metaphors on full moon nights.
He made poetry with Southey and Coleridge,
used verse to express his science.

Thrilled through his limbs, his hands and feet,
he inhaled nitrous oxide gas,
testing its power to anaesthetize
and found a new pleasure
for which common language has no name,
thoughts springing up like turf beneath his feet,
the tones of Aeolian harps ringing in his head.
Instead he laughed and, like a madman,
danced around, wrote a poem.

My writing notebook of scribbles and dashes
is his oiled silk bag filled with gases,
the experimental places where the invisible is stored.
Poetic science shines in packets of light,
my words float and spin in unexpected order.
It's a melange of the senses in a theatre
where quirky Davy is master of ceremonies.
When I write, sometimes the universe vibrates.

# Two Hour Prescription

Bats flit; the ruined tower is theirs.
Kingfisher flirts sapphire by the burn,
heron stalk-still on a rock. Leaf kittle.
Pale yellow pines wave from the white.
Slow wander on the woodland floor,
settle on a log. Sink into its aged strength.
Spot roe deer slip by, stop to stare at you.
Stroke seasoned bark, its roughness,
cracks and fissures. Soak up the oxygen,
rich brown stained cherry, chocolate walnut burls,
red-brown cedar knotted trunk, white dotted brown ash,
patterned cream birch. Sunlight blinking,
birds calling *human*. Forest bathe.
Let breath rise from your core.

# The Tree of Tales

I am Scots pine, ancient-wild-evergreen,
immortal marker, Dalguise legend. I reign supreme.
Plant my sweet scent beneath summer skies.
I am Scots pine, ancient-wild-evergreen,
once was a god's cone-tipped wand, an amulet.
Now I'm in a pact with human, glen and rivulet.
I am Scots pine, ancient-wild-evergreen,
immortal marker, Kingussie legend. I reign supreme.

# Fitch

In my midnight I unhook the dust-framed painting,
a childhood spook, a haunting, a fur mask,
and suddenly there's a polecat,
her coat a silkscreen print, soft as her starlit complexion,
the dark patches blotted. She is our solitary hunter.
From the gloam of a sand dune, out of oils,
she slouches. Musk charges the room.

She is my mother, returned to seek out
her ghost husband, reclaiming him,
he, who was always leafing in libraries.
She drags him by the scruff of his neck,
flicking her tail in the scramble over rockery and log pile.

By dawn she is back in the kitchen,
wielding an iron, as a wife might, pressing office shirts.
I rise to the taste of the polecat's low mewling to her mate.

# The Glaistig

We please her at the gloaming by the pond
with a pool of milk in a millstone cradle,
not warm at all or scorn-boiled.
Solstice, all seasons, each generation.

We flatten against the standing stone,
never knowing how she might appear,
always in her favoured green,
plaid wafting in Atlantic surge,
or what her mood might be,
grey or blue or gold.

We wait for the wailing or the tricks or her
fixing on our scent. Dragonflies and moths
hover on her heartbeat. Deer dart into the ether,
a distant fiddler strums a jig through the indigo.

# Cailleach

Plaided in grey-white, the Hag drops
rock-mountains before my foot-stumble.
I pay no heed, climb through my black dog mist
into the spit of tight-jawed spectres.
On the valley floor
doors swing ajar.
Hisses and jibes lurch in cloud hems.

On a second winter-wilderness day
her hammer pounds stepping stones,
her staff freezes the ground.

Love is a needle threaded with pain
and secret vows, blunted
in the flash of an instant.
My map is weathered, peppered with holes.

I crawl
into gaps
between boulders.

The Winter Queen battles rebirth,
invokes sleet storms, hunts songbirds and hedgerow.
I slip through green spring and maple autumn,
nurse my heart into middle March.

In summer Moor scatters
bloodless heather, spread tight, white on grey rock,
as pure as Malvina's tears on her wedding day.
Mine were tears of joy, the growing up sense of it all
but love has broken away,
one wing of the raptor gone.

I turn towards the river's shimmer,
its current a moving smile as light intensifies.

# The Ceasg's Ghazal

Love at first sight, the fisherman cries me his heart's desire,
for this human adores my salmon tail, his watery heart's desire.

Through the loch's green he spies my splash, the bubbles of lust
buoyant with three wishes granted, my beloved heart's desire.

First, to shapeshift as mortal, second, be his all our mortal days,
third, to bear his child in human form, our hearts' consuming
    desire.

My crazed sister, goddess of the sea, insists my love be blood
    sacrifice.
Hunted-haunted as prey, I fought to save my earth angel, my
    heart's desire.

Horror struck, my othery monster sister murders my love in a
    foamy rage,
precious fisher-father to my maritime boy, deepest ocean heart's
    desire.

Our only born sails to the world's end, nets thickened with fishes,
through monsoon and hurricane. I spell-cast shields for my heart's
    desire.

I am Ceasg, singer of lament, of beauty, maid of the wave,
keeper of maritime souls, mourner of earthly things, craving my
    heart's desire.

# About the Author

Maggie Mackay loves family history, which she incorporates into work in print, anthologies and online journals. She is a Poetry Masters Graduate of The Writing School, Manchester Metropolitan University. Her poem appears in the award-winning *#MeToo* anthology. Others have been nominated for The Forward Prize, Best Single Poem, with one commended in the Mothers' Milk Writing Prize. Her pamphlet 'The Heart of the Run' is published by Picaroon Poetry and the booklet 'Sweet Chestnut' published by Karen Little in aid of animal welfare. She is a reviewer for https://www.sphinxreview.co.uk/.

Thanks to Maureen Cullen, always, for her insightful advice and to everyone in my life who has encouraged my writing over recent years. You know who you are.

Kelsay Books

Printed in Great Britain
by Amazon

54710336R00047